Teens in PERU

by Sandy Donovan

Content Adviser: Jose Javier Lopez, Ph.D.,
Professor, Department of Geography,
Minnesota State University, Mankato

Reading Adviser: Alexa L. Sandmann, Ed.D.,
Professor of Literacy, College and
Graduate School of Education,
Kent State University

Compass Point Books ✦ Minneapolis, Minnesota

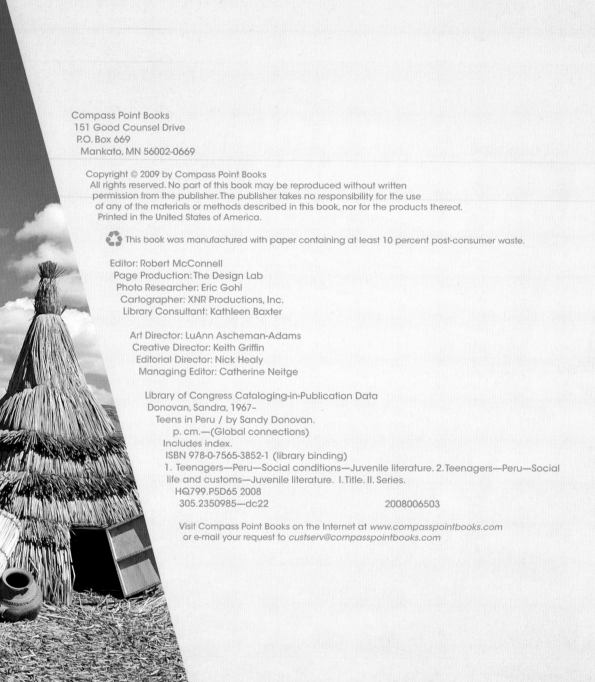

Compass Point Books
151 Good Counsel Drive
P.O. Box 669
Mankato, MN 56002-0669

This book was manufactured with paper containing at least 10 percent post-consumer waste.

Editor: Robert McConnell
Page Production: The Design Lab
Photo Researcher: Eric Gohl
Cartographer: XNR Productions, Inc.
Library Consultant: Kathleen Baxter

Art Director: LuAnn Ascheman-Adams
Creative Director: Keith Griffin
Editorial Director: Nick Healy
Managing Editor: Catherine Neitge

Library of Congress Cataloging-in-Publication Data
Donovan, Sandra, 1967–
  Teens in Peru / by Sandy Donovan.
     p. cm.—(Global connections)
  Includes index.
  ISBN 978-0-7565-3852-1 (library binding)
  1. Teenagers—Peru—Social conditions—Juvenile literature. 2. Teenagers—Peru—Social
life and customs—Juvenile literature. I. Title. II. Series.
  HQ799.P5D65 2008
    305.2350985—dc22   2008006503

Visit Compass Point Books on the Internet at www.compasspointbooks.com
or e-mail your request to custserv@compasspointbooks.com

Table of Contents

PACIFIC
OCEAN

MEXICO

⭐ Lima

TES OF AMERICA

**ATLANTIC
OCEAN**

THE BAHAMAS

CUBA

HAITI DOM. REP.

JAMAICA

BELIZE

GUATEMALA

HONDURAS

EL SALVADOR   NICARAGUA

COSTA RICA   PANAMA

VENEZUELA

FRENCH GUIANA

GUYANA

SURINAME

COLOMBIA

ECUADOR

PERÚ

BRAZIL

BOLIVIA

CHILE   PARAGUAY

TEENS IN PERÚ

TEENS IN PERU LIVE VASTLY DIFFERENT LIVES, depending on their family's position in society. Teens from low-income families, who tend to be descendants of Peru's indigenous tribes, lead difficult but meaningful lives. They experience poverty and hard work, but their lives are rich in family and culture. They generally live in the rural highlands or in shantytowns in coastal cities.

Teens from upper-income families are often descendants of the Spanish who explored, conquered, and settled in Peru beginning in the 1500s. These teens lead sheltered lives and have many modern conveniences. They attend private schools and often find jobs in a family business.

Peru's upper- and lower-income teens rarely cross paths. But they do share a respect for their country's traditions and a love of family. And in a country where one in three people is a teenager and the median age is just 25, all of Peru's teens carry a big responsibility to preserve their rich traditions and family connections, as well as to move their country forward.

City students often wear uniforms, but they might add special items for events such as parades.

CHAPTER ONE

Crowded Classrooms

SEATED AROUND A HEAVY WOODEN TABLE in a one-room adobe brick schoolhouse, 20 young Peruvians practice spelling in Spanish. These 12- and 13-year-olds live high in the Andes Mountains. Growing up, they learned to speak their native language, Quechua. In elementary school, they learned to read and write in Quechua. Now, in secondary school, they are learning Spanish, Peru's main language for business and government.

The Peruvian government provides free education at four levels. The first level is preschool, and about half of all children ages 3 to 5 attend. The second level begins at either kindergarten or first grade and goes through sixth grade. Some children start kindergarten at age 5, but more begin in first grade at about age 6. Primary school is required for children from age 6 to about 12. The third and fourth levels are lower secondary school and upper secondary school, for ages 12 to 16. Although the attendance rate for lower secondary school is very high (95 percent), it drops abruptly (to 77 percent) for upper secondary school. Fewer girls than boys attend secondary

Reading and Writing

Literacy is defined as the proportion of citizens 15 years old and older who can read and write. Peru's literacy rate of 88 percent is comparable to the rates of most other countries in South America.

Population	Literacy Rate
All Peruvians	88%
Male Peruvians	94%
Female Peruvians	82%

Source: United States Central Intelligence Agency. *The World Factbook—Peru.*

school. Still, a 77 percent enrollment rate is high for a poor country like Peru.

However, government requirements and high enrollment rates do not tell the whole story. As with many things in Peru, school experiences vary greatly. Schools in rural areas are quite different from city schools. Even within cities, students from poor families have vastly different school experiences than those of students from wealthier families.

Rural Schools

Most teenagers in rural Peru try to go to school as much as they can. Their families are almost always farmers who work hard to grow enough food to survive. During planting and harvest seasons, teens often have to miss school in order to help at home. Boys usually work with male relatives in the fields. Girls usually help cook, clean, and take care of younger and older family members.

Students in some rural areas go to school in the shadow of the Andes Mountains.

Rural Peruvian families value education. Educating children is a source of pride for families and villages. It also is seen as a pathway to a better life. Nearly every small village of at least 200 people has an *escuelita*—a little school. These schools have kindergarten and primary grades, usually in one room. Teens can attend the local secondary school, but it may be far away. This is one reason many rural Peruvians drop out of school after finishing the primary grades.

Children and teens in particularly remote areas are served by a system of *núcleos*. A núcleo

escuelita
ES-kwah-LEE-tah

núcleos
NOO-klee-ohs

Respect for Learning

The Peruvian government lacks the money needed to provide enough schools and teachers to serve the entire young population. This means many teenagers cannot go beyond primary school. However, education and learning in general are greatly respected in Peru. In fact, the names and hometowns of all college graduates are regularly announced in the newspapers.

For many years, the country even had a law that banned teachers from holding government offices such as mayor or council member. The thought behind the law was that citizens respected teachers so much that a teacher in public office would have too much influence on public matters. The law no longer exists, but all Peruvian teachers are still held in high esteem.

is a central school that provides all levels of education—kindergarten, primary, and secondary. Teens and their younger siblings may walk or ride several miles to reach their núcleos. It is common for teens who live a long way from the nearest school to stay overnight at the homes of family friends.

Peru is buying low-cost laptop computers for pupils in 9,000 elementary schools through an international program.

These are groups formed by people who originally might have come from a small village but now live in a city and make enough money to help the village.

Many núcleos have only one room. Teenagers might group around a small table to learn to read and write in Spanish. Across the room, younger children—often siblings of the teens—might gather with their own teacher to learn to read and write in their native language. A secondary school in a provincial capital may be in a larger building. Sometimes the buildings are European-style structures built by the Spanish, who conquered Peru in the 1500s.

In either type of rural school, the students might only have a few textbooks to share. They are sent by the Peruvian government. Apart from learning to read and write in Spanish, students focus on Peruvian history. They learn about Peru's difficult past relationships with its neighbors, the countries of Chile and Ecuador. They learn about the lives of Peruvian national heroes, such as Admiral Miguel Grau, Colonel Francisco Bolognesi, and Leoncio Prado, who were all killed in battles with Chile. Festivities honoring these heroes are part of every school year. Some critics claim that Peruvian schools teach their students to mistrust all Chilean people because of the two countries' rocky history.

Students in rural Peru wear their everyday clothes to school—usually

Núcleos and escuelitas are usually made of adobe—earthen bricks that have been baked in the sun. Often a whole village works together to make the adobe and build the school. Sometimes the government provides the money to build the school, but sometimes it comes from private associations.

Spanish is the language spoken by most teens in urban schools.

Western-style cotton pants and shirts. Every once in a while a student comes to school in a navy blue and white school uniform. This is most likely a hand-me-down gift from a relative who has moved to a city, where school uniforms are common.

Schools in the City

Wearing uniforms is not the only way that school life in the cities differs from school life in rural areas. Most urban teens grow up speaking Spanish. Some families that recently moved from the countryside speak Quechua or another native Peruvian language. But beginning in kindergarten, Spanish is the language taught in schools. Also, urban schools are fairly close to students' homes. This helps explain why urban teens usually attend school for more years than teens in rural areas.

An urban teenager's life is shaped by the social class of his or her family.

Social class is based on both ethnic background and wealth. Most Peruvian city residents are either native Peruvians or mestizos—people of mixed native and Spanish descent. Most city residents have very low incomes. Teens from these families attend public schools. They often wear military-style uniforms of navy pants or skirts, white shirts, and

Two Official Languages

For centuries after the Spanish conquered Peru, Spanish was the country's official language. But more than a dozen other languages, including about 100 dialects, are spoken by Peruvians.

In 1975, Peruvian law made one of these languages, Quechua, a second national language. Indigenous people of the Andes highlands often speak Quechua, the language of the Incas. Most of the country's 10 million Quechua speakers also can speak

Spanish, but about one-fourth of them speak only their native language. Quechua is the most commonly spoken native American language, and many English words—such as puma, condor, and llama—are Quechua words.

In southern Peru, near Lake Titicaca, some people speak Aymará, the language of the native Aymará people. In the Amazon River basin, there are 12 language families. But there are few remaining speakers of any of these languages.

Life is hard in Lima's shantytowns, and even young children might have to carry water home and do other chores.

navy caps. Sometimes they wear their everyday clothing—jeans, cotton pants or skirts, and cotton shirts.

An urban school might be a Spanish colonial building in the city's historic center or a ramshackle building made quickly and cheaply of wood and tin. In either case, it is likely to be overcrowded. Peru's population explosion means there are more students than there is room for them in school. Teachers can also be hard to find, and the low pay makes it hard to attract the best teachers. Often teachers with college degrees in one area end up teaching all subjects.

Teen Scenes

In rural Peru, high in the Andes Mountains, a 15-year-old boy wakes up in his family's one-room house. He rolls up his small bedding mat and turns on the family's battery-powered radio. It is the one thing that connects his remote home to the rest of the world. As he listens to news from neighboring villages, he dresses for a day in the fields. He will spend the day helping his father, brother, and other relatives harvest the potato crop. Until he was 12, he attended school at the local escuelita, but lately his family has needed his help at home. He hopes to move to Lima one day and get a job that he thinks will be easier than his long workdays in the mountains.

Meanwhile, in Lima, another 15-year-old begins her day. She wakes up in her own bedroom and turns on her sound system. Downstairs the family cook is preparing breakfast, and the teen takes her time choosing what she will wear to school. Since her school is several miles from her family's home, she will get a ride there and back.

In one of Lima's sprawling slums, another 15-year-old girl is also getting ready for school. First she helps her mother fill a large bucket of water from the local water faucet. She hauls this to the family's two-room apartment in a crumbling cinder-block building. She is eager to get to school, but first she has to help her mother prepare breakfast. Then, using the water they carried back, they will wash the few dishes and sweep out the apartment. She rushes through this work so she can meet a friend in time for them to walk to school together.

School uniforms often mean that the students wearing them are from families with little income.

Courses include Spanish literature, history, math, and science. And just as in rural schools, there is a great emphasis on nationalism—the celebration of loyalty and devotion to Peru. For instance, in Lima each year, high school students spend months preparing for a huge Independence Day parade through the city. In their uniforms, the students look like military cadets.

The overcrowded classrooms and underskilled teachers in many Peruvian schools lead most urban families that can afford it to send their children to

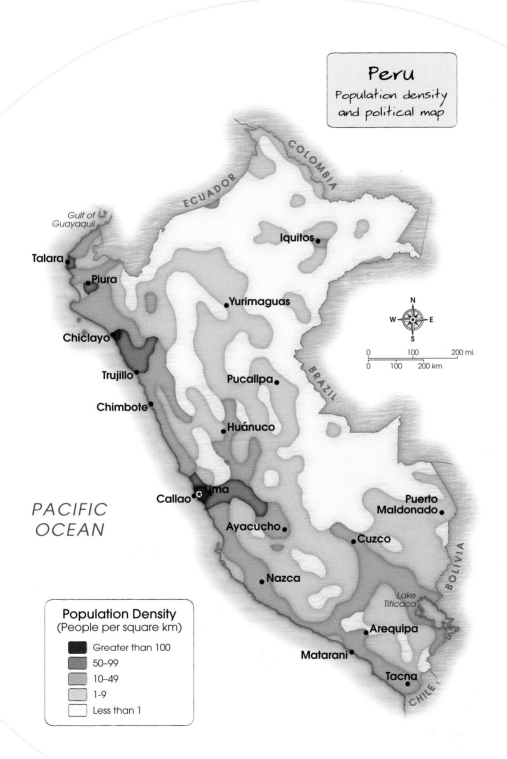

Peru
Population density
and political map

COLOMBIA

ECUADOR

Gulf of
Guayaquil

Talara

Piura

Chiclayo

Trujillo

Chimbote

Iquitos

Yurimaguas

BRAZIL

Pucallpa

Huánuco

N
W   E
S

0   100   200 mi.
0   100   200 km

PACIFIC
OCEAN

Callao • Lima

Ayacucho

Nazca

Puerto
Maldonado

Cuzco

BOLIVIA

Lake
Titicaca

Arequipa

Matarani

Tacna

CHILE

Population Density
(People per square km)

- Greater than 100
- 50–99
- 10–49
- 1-9
- Less than 1

private schools. Most middle- and high-income Peruvians live in Lima or Trujillo, and most of them have mestizo or Spanish backgrounds. Teens from these families are likely to attend private schools. Middle-income families send their children to local private schools, which are sometimes connected to the Roman Catholic Church. Students study Spanish-language literature, Latin American and European history, math, biology, chemistry, geography, and physics.

Many wealthy families send their teens to boarding schools in Europe or the United States. This boosts the families' social status and helps to ensure that the students can get into a foreign college or university. Both middle- and upper-income teens are far more likely than poor urban or rural teens to graduate from secondary school and go on to college.

After High School

Peruvian teens finish secondary school at about age 16. But although 77 percent of all Peruvian teens enter secondary school, only about 55 percent graduate. Almost all private school students graduate, while few rural students do. Rural students often start working full time before finishing secondary school. Still, Peru is making progress toward educating more of its young people. Although only 55 percent of young adults (ages 20 to 24) have graduated from high school, this rate

Some Peruvian college students find time for such political activities as protests.

The University of San Marcos, in Lima, draws many students from middle-class families.

is higher than ever. Only 21 percent of older Peruvians (ages 55 to 64) have high school diplomas.

For teens who graduate from secondary schools, Peru offers a variety of colleges and universities. There are more than 30 public universities and 10 major private universities. In fact, the oldest continually operating university in the Americas is in Peru—the University of San Marcos opened in Lima in 1551 and is still operating.

Teens and young adults from middle-income families tend to go to these universities to study to become professors, doctors, lawyers, engineers, and other professionals. Many teens from wealthy families go to universities in Europe or the United States. It is still rare for a young adult from rural Peru to attend college. But those who earn a college degree are greatly respected in their home villages.

Shantytowns or slums are home to nearly all teens who live in the urban areas of Peru.

CHAPTER TWO

From Huts to High-Rises

TEENAGERS' DAILY LIVES IN PERU VARY GREATLY, depending mostly on where they live and how much money their families have. Teens in rural Peru—in the Andes or Sierra mountains or in the Amazon River valley—tend to live much the way their ancestors did. Urban teens are much more affected by modern culture. They enjoy more modern conveniences, such as television. However, they also live with modern problems, such as crowded and dirty neighborhoods.

In Peru's larger cities, teenagers spill out of schools at about 3 P.M. They enter the already crowded streets for their journeys home. Three-fourths of all Peruvians live in cities, and about one-third live in Lima, the capital. For several decades, rural Peruvians have been moving to the cities. The urban population is growing so fast that cities' housing, roads, sewers, and garbage collection can't keep up with the demand.

Nearly 95 percent of urban teens live in shanty-towns in city outskirts or in slums in city centers. In the shantytowns, people build housing out of whatever

25

Rural Violence and Migration

For several decades, deadly violence has terrified people in many parts of rural Peru. The violence has two causes: terrorism and illegal drug traffic. Terrorist groups are trying to take over the government, and they use deadly bombings and other violence to achieve this goal.

One of the largest groups has been Shining Path, which aimed to replace the government with a communist society in which farmers and workers have fairer shares of the nation's resources. During its heyday in the 1980s and early 1990s, Shining Path used terror to frighten government leaders and was responsible for tens of thousands of deaths across Peru.

Other deadly violence stems from the large illegal cocaine industry. Cocaine, a narcotic drug, is made from the coca plant, which grows throughout the Peruvian highlands. The drug can be sold for a lot of money on the illegal international drug market. The Peruvian government has tried to crack down on the illegal drug trade by burning coca fields, among other efforts. But drug traffickers, because there is so much money at stake, often use violence to protect their illegal activity.

To escape this violence in their communities, thousands of rural Peruvians began moving to Lima and other large cities along the coast. But the lives they have there are hardly better than the violence they left behind. They are crowded into slums and often cannot find jobs or health care. They live without electricity and running water and have no access to safe drinking water.

materials they can find—cardboard, bricks, bamboo, and even cloth. A seven-member family might live in one small room with no running water or electricity. Teens who live here typically spend much of their day helping to take care of the family.

Girls and their mothers may get up early to haul buckets of water from the nearest water tap. The water is used for washing and cooking over makeshift stoves. When the daily chores are done, girls might go to school. But they also

might be needed to help take care of younger children or help their mothers with odd jobs, such as selling small items on street corners. Boys often get up early with their fathers to take a long bus ride to a construction site, where they work as daily laborers. The work is hard, pays little, and often is dangerous. Safety equipment, such as goggles and steel-toed boots, is rare.

The lives of middle- and upper-income urban teens are vastly different from those of their low-income peers. In

Many middle- and upper-income teens live in high-rise apartments.

fact, they share little other than a common language and, almost always, a love for their country. Almost all middle- and upper-income teens spend their days in school and their afternoons taking part in after-school activities, such as music or sports. They live in high-rise apartments or single-family houses. Middle-income families take great pride in their homes, and a European-style single-family residence is a sign of

social status. Teenagers in these homes have their own bedrooms, which are equipped with stereos, televisions, and DVD players. The wealthiest families have at least one other home, often in a city along the coast.

At Home in the Mountains

A teen living on a farm high in the Andes or Sierra mountains probably begins her day before the sun comes

Many Peruvian farm families own little and live much the way their ancestors did.

At Home in the Amazon

Some Peruvian teens live in the basin of the Amazon River, east of the Andes Mountains. Fewer than 10 percent of Peruvians live there. Like the rural residents of Peru's mountainous areas, they live a simple life similar to that of their ancestors. Teenage girls learn how to grow bananas, yuca (a starchy root vegetable), sugarcane, and cacao, which is used to make chocolate, soap, and chewing gum. Teenage boys learn to hunt wild pigs, deer, and monkeys.

Extended families of 30 to 40 people live together in large houses. The houses have poles to keep them high off the ground in case of floods. They often have no walls but are covered with a thatched roof made of palm. This open style makes the area's hot, humid climate more bearable. Under the roof, families gather on wooden floors and benches. Hammocks are strung from the poles, allowing sleepers to catch as much of a breeze as they can.

In the Amazon region of Peru, many teen girls have to take care of their younger brothers and sisters.

up. She may help her mother prepare mate, an herbal tea, for the family. If it's planting or harvesting season, the entire family will wake early and have a cup of mate sweetened with sugar. Along with this, they'll have a light meal of bread or *mote*, a kind of cereal made of dried corn.

mote
MO-tay

Fewer than one-fourth of Peruvians live in the country's mountainous rural areas. Families there typically have homes with just one or two rooms. The homes have adobe walls and roofs of either thatched grass or tile. Some have an attic under the roof where they keep dried food for the winter. The floors are dirt. The families have few possessions. The poorest families lay wool blankets on the floor for sleeping. They might have no furniture and only a fireplace for cooking and heat. Some families have a few pieces of furniture: perhaps a couple of stools, a bed frame, and a dried-grass mattress. Male family members sit on the stools at meals; the rest of the family crouches around a mat to eat. They have no table.

In many ways, these homes look like rural Peruvian homes hundreds of years ago. None has running water or electricity. Very few modern tools are found in many Andes homes today. Most families have metal pots and pans for cooking, and most have farm tools. Often the prized possessions are a radio and batteries. With a radio, families living in remote areas can receive news from other parts of the country. Mountain broadcasts can include several hours of messages from one village to another. A family member who has moved to a town or city may send word

that he or she is coming for a visit. Weather reports are also popular.

A teenager's life in the mountains is full of hard work, especially during growing seasons. Boys work in the fields with their fathers and other male relatives. Teenage girls usually make meals with female relatives. First they prepare a large breakfast of potato and vegetable stew. After this meal, the men and boys head out to the fields. The women prepare lunch, which they will carry to the fields. This is the largest meal of the day, and it includes meat, if any is available. After lunch, a teenage girl might remain in the fields to help with planting or harvesting. Or she might return home to help clean up, tend to the family's chickens and pigs, or take care of younger siblings.

Mealtime

In cities, such as Lima, it's not uncommon to see a crowd of teenagers gathered at a fast-food restaurant such as McDonald's after school. While with their friends, middle- and upper-income teens eat hamburgers, french fries, pizza, and other snack foods familiar to teens around the world. They also buy food from the street vendors that are common in Peruvian cities. The vendors sell local food, such as skewers of grilled meat or fish. Teens can also grab a sweet treat, such as an Italian-style shaved ice. But at home they are more likely to sit down to a traditional meal with their families. Peru's mountains,

31

Many Peruvians stop to sample the foods grilled by street vendors.

rivers, and coastal areas provide a huge variety of flavorful ingredients for the country's many cooking styles. What's on the dinner table varies across Peru.

Teens living in the highlands tend to eat meals of potatoes, corn, and chili peppers—the same foods their ancestors grew for centuries. Each family might grow dozens of varieties of each of these vegetables and use them for soups

and stews. Spicy peppers range in color from red to orange to yellow, and they also vary in spiciness, from relatively mild to mouth-burning hot.

Whenever available, meat is grilled or added to soups and stews for protein. The most common meat in the highlands is beef, which is eaten in many countries. But another favorite meat is unique to Peru: guinea pig. In the high-

National Food Staple

Potatoes are often called the national food of Peru, although many wealthy Peruvians consider them food for the poor. Potatoes grow particularly well in the Andes Mountains, where more than 200 varieties are planted and harvested. *Papas*, as they are called in Spanish, are valued by farming families because they can easily be freeze-dried—without electricity—and stored for up to four years.

papas
pah-pahs

Farmers lay them out on the cold ground, and when the temperature dips below freezing at night, the potatoes begin to freeze. The next day, as the temperature rises, they begin to thaw, and then they are frozen more the next night. This cycle is repeated for several nights until they are completely dry and like cardboard. Then they are stored for later use.

A favorite way to prepare potatoes is as an appetizer called Papas a la Huancaína:

• 10 medium potatoes (new potatoes are best)
• 1 pound cheese
• 2 small hot peppers
• 1 cup evaporated milk
• ½ cup vegetable oil
• 2 cloves garlic
• ¼ cup coarsely ground flour
• 1 teaspoon prepared mustard
• Salt and pepper
• Lettuce
• 3 hard-cooked eggs
• Black olives (optional)

Cook and peel the potatoes and allow them to cool. In a blender, blend the cheese, peppers, milk, oil, garlic, flour, mustard, salt, and pepper. The sauce should be fairly thick; add flour if it's not thick enough, or add milk if it's too thick. Lay a bed of lettuce in a serving dish and place the potatoes on top. Cover with the sauce. Cut the eggs in half and place on top of the potatoes. Add black olives, if desired.

lands, families breed their own guinea pigs, and the rodents are fried, roasted, grilled, or cut up for a stew.

Other popular dishes are *rocoto relleno*, which are spicy peppers stuffed with ground beef and vegetables, and tamales, which are made of cornmeal and beans or beef, wrapped in corn husks. Sometimes food is cooked in an underground oven. A family or even a whole village digs a hole and lights a fire at the bottom of it. They place large flat stones on top of the fire. When the stones are hot, they cook meat or vegetables on them.

In the Amazon River valley, teenagers also tend to eat traditional meals that they help prepare. Dishes in this part of the country are less spicy,

rocoto relleno
roh-KOH-toh ray-YAY-noh

Guinea pigs are pets in other parts of the world, but in Peru they are a food source.

Ronda Criolla is a dish that might be on the menu of a city restaurant in Peru.

yuca
YOU-kuh

juanes
HWAH-nays

criolla
kree-YOH-lah

and they include more fish—fresh from the Amazon River. Many families grow *yuca*, a starchlike vegetable similar to a potato. The area's thick jungles contain thousands of kinds of animals that can be hunted. Family meals include crops they have grown, fish they have caught, and meat they have hunted. A favorite meal is *juanes*, which is fish or chicken and yuca, steamed in a banana leaf.

The cuisine along the coast and in most of Peru's cities is called *criolla*. It's a mixture of the cooking styles of indigenous Peruvians and those of the Spanish conquerors. Criolla food is spicy hot and often features meat or fish cooked with tomatoes, onions, garlic, and peppers. Chicken and goat are the most common meats along the coast. Fresh fruits, such as pineapples, bananas, and oranges, are plentiful. A favorite criolla dish is Aji de Gallina,

Different Lifestyles

What's on the mind of Peruvian teens has a lot to do with their families' wealth. The differences were explained by an upper-income 18-year-old who was interviewed for the U.S. TV program *The NewsHour With Jim Lehrer*:

For the upper class [Peruvian teens], the most important thing is probably being a fulfilled human being, developing a holistic and well-balanced lifestyle that includes education and recreation. For the middle-class youth, the most important thing is probably an education, and they must therefore also find a job to afford it. The lower class must worry about more basic things like getting food and shelter. They are many times responsible for their large families at a very young age. ...

I am fortunate enough to be among the few privileged teenagers who have very little transcendental [major] worries. I worry about the test I have next week, and that I didn't have time to go to the gym today, that my parents argued, or my sister had an accident. But as I have mentioned before, other people my age, in this same city, have much greater responsibilities.

Teens can sell flattened cans to earn money for their families.

The popularity of Inca Kola practically makes it the national soft drink of Peru.

which is chicken cooked in a spicy sauce of peppers and chili paste, together with evaporated milk, boiled potatoes, and hard-boiled eggs. *Aji* is also the name of Peru's most used condiment, a spicy sauce of hot peppers and lemon juice or vegetable oil.

At least once a day, many teens reach for their favorite drink, Inca Kola. This fruity, gold-colored carbonated drink is very popular. Its taste has been described as "liquid bubble gum." Other soft drinks, such as Coca-Cola and Pepsi, are also available. Older teens and their parents often drink *chicha*, a beer made of fermented corn, with their meals. Favorite Peruvian desserts include cakes and cookies filled with cream or fruit.

aji
AH-hee

chicha
CHEE-cha

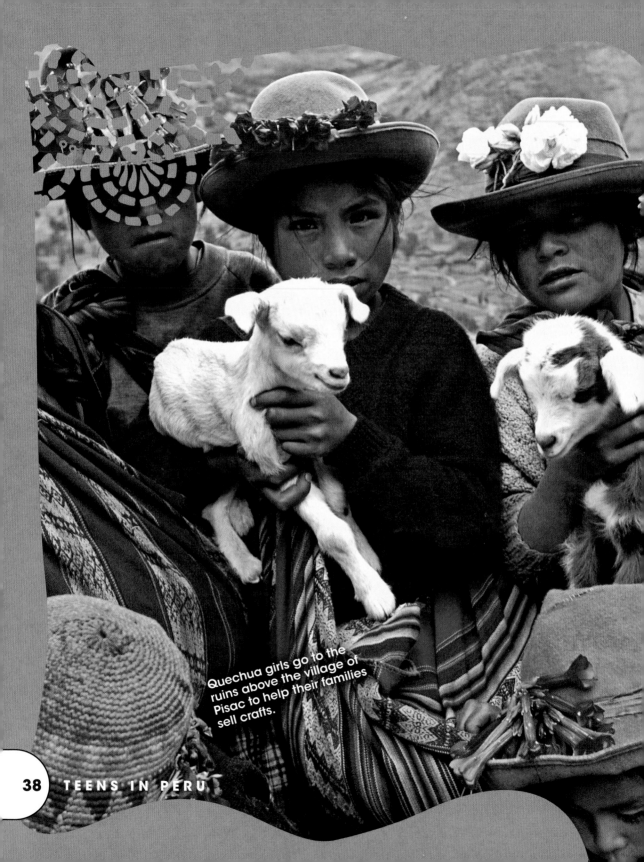

Quechua girls go to the ruins above the village of Pisac to help their families sell crafts.

3

Friendships & Family Life

FAMILY IS AT THE CENTER OF EVERY PERUVIAN TEEN'S SOCIAL WORLD. Many teens hang out with friends at school and during free time, but their family ties are their most important relationships. The makeup of families varies, depending on income and race, as well as where the family lives.

Teens whose families are either direct Spanish descendants or Spanish-speaking mestizos usually grow up in traditional, male-dominated families. These families live in coastal areas and in larger cities. A family usually consists of a father, a mother, and two to three children. While grandparents, cousins, aunts, and uncles are a big part of a teen's life, they do not usually live in the same house.

The Hispanic concept of *machismo* is strong among Spanish-speaking Peruvians. Machismo is the attitude that males are superior to women.

machismo
mah-SHEES-moh

A family on Isla Amantani, an island in Lake Titicaca, posed for a portrait. There are many American Indian villages near the shore of the lake.

Across the Spanish-speaking world, men take great pride in their machismo. Peruvian men are no exception. They pride themselves on being strong, capable, and in charge. Machismo has many negative effects. Women are expected to defer to men and are often not allowed to object to bad behavior by men. But machismo also has a positive influence: Men feel a strong responsibility to care for their families.

Fathers are the most important

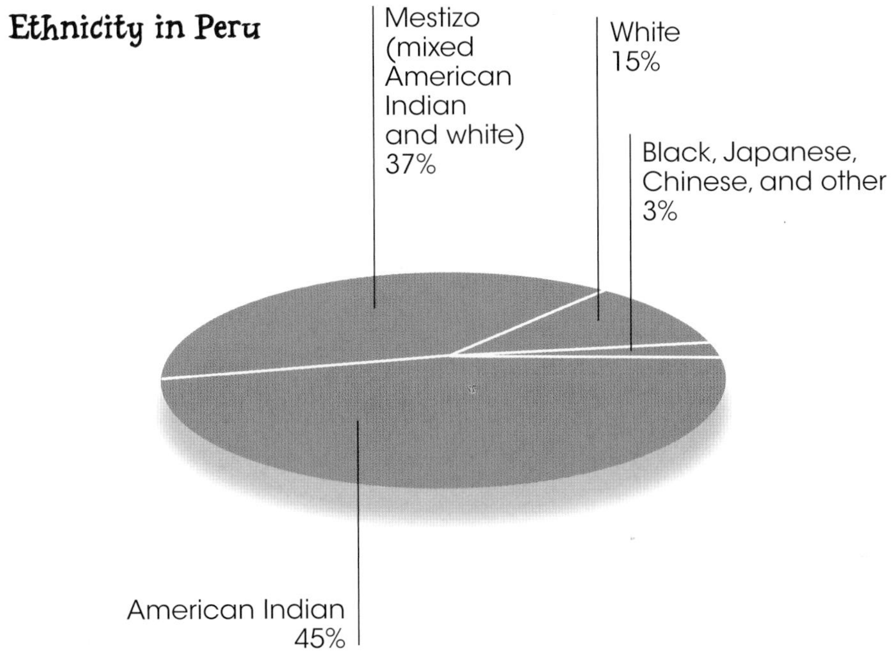

Ethnicity in Peru

Mestizo
(mixed
American
Indian
and white)
37%

White
15%

Black, Japanese,
Chinese, and other
3%

American Indian
45%

Source: United States Central Intelligence Agency.
The World Factbook—Peru.

members of these families. Until recently, they provided the family's sole financial support. They are in charge of the family's money. They also handle discipline and can be quite strict with their children. Among siblings, the oldest brother is considered the leader. He inherits most of the father's estate and takes over as head of the family when his father dies.

Traditionally, mothers have been in charge of children's education. They also manage the household tasks, which in almost all middle- and upper-income families involves overseeing servants. Increasingly, though, mothers are taking jobs outside the home. Some women

Ethnic Groups

Although life in Peru differs greatly based on where people live and how much money they have, Peruvians define themselves first by their ethnicity.

The country's largest ethnic group—about 45 percent of all Peruvians—is indigenous American Indians. The largest groups of indigenous Peruvians live in the Andes highlands. They are the Quechuas, who are descendants of the Incas, and the Aymarás. In the past several decades, many highlands natives have moved to cities in search of better lives. There they have begun to marry Peruvians of mixed Spanish and native ethnicity. Smaller groups of indigenous Peruvians live in the Amazon rain forests. These tribes include the Yaguas and the Machiguengas. They tend to live in isolation and rarely marry—or even meet—people of other ethnic groups.

The next-largest ethnic group—about 37 percent of all Peruvians—is the mestizos, who have indigenous and Spanish ancestry. The mestizos live primarily along the coast and in cities. Having Spanish ancestors is considered a mark of superiority, and the more Spanish blood a mestizo family has, the higher its social status. There is even a name—*cholos*—for Peruvians with mostly indigenous blood who want to be considered mestizos. Cholos tend to live in slums or shantytowns and want to join the middle-income class. As mestizos, they would be established as middle class and probably would live in newer apartment buildings or single-family houses.

cholos
CHOH-lohs

The most elite group of Peruvians—about 15 percent—are descendants of the Spanish conquistadores. They tend to be lighter-skinned than most mestizos or indigenous Peruvians. The Spanish Peruvians have formed a closed society, and they control most of government and business. Middle-level managers in government and business are almost always mestizo. Although mestizos might advance professionally, they will never be considered part of the elite if they have too much indigenous blood.

American Indians, such as a Yagua family in the Amazon region, are the largest ethnic group in Peru.

who separate from their husbands are even assuming the role of head of household.

Many young adults still defer to their fathers. Only young adults from the wealthiest families move out to live on their own. Both sons and daughters usually live with their parents until they marry—often in their mid-20s. Even after marriage, many young couples keep living with their parents. Once

they have children—and earn enough money—they move into their own house or apartment. Still, they continue to be entwined in the lives of their parents and adult siblings, often seeing them every day.

Native Traditions

For teens growing up in rural Peru—the descendants of the Incas and other American Indians—family is also at the center of their world. But these families have traditions that are different from those of Spanish-speaking families.

In the highlands, teenagers generally live with their parents and siblings. Their closest neighbors are their grandparents, aunts, uncles, and cousins. By the time children are in their late teens, their parents may have begun to arrange a marriage for them. Unlike the custom in some societies, though, young adults do not have to accept their parents' choice of marriage partner.

Once an arrangement is proposed, the couple begins a trial marriage. The young man works with his father-in-law, and the young woman works with her mother-in-law. The couple might live together, and with the young husband's parents, during this period. They usually do not formally marry, though, until they have at least one child.

Native Discrimination

Even though nearly half of Peruvians are native American Indians, this ethnic group faces a lot of discrimination in Peru. People with any Spanish blood look down on indigenous Peruvians, and the word *Indian* is often used as an insult. Native Peruvians hold few top business or government positions.

The government has made some effort to outlaw discrimination. In the 1970s, it briefly became illegal to use *Indian* to describe indigenous people. Today the term is no longer outlawed, but indigenous people like the Quechua and the Aymará are officially called peasants instead of Indians.

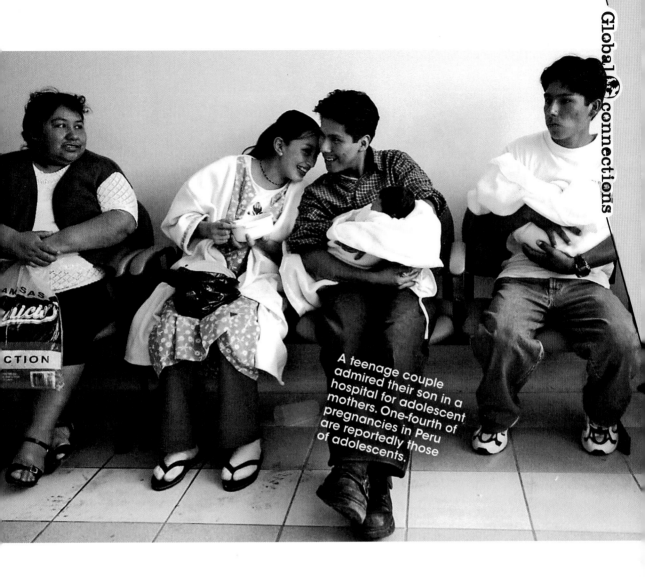

A teenage couple admired their son in a hospital for adolescent mothers. One-fourth of pregnancies in Peru are reportedly those of adolescents.

Among the Quechua, it is not uncommon for couples to end a marriage. Women or men can decide to do this, and even for women—unlike in Hispanic culture—no stigma is attached to divorce. Even after a woman has children, she can leave her husband and marry another man. Children of the divorced couple often are brought up by the entire village.

Traditionally, rural families were larger than urban families. Many had five or six children. But recently the average size of rural families has dropped to 4.9 people, or about three children per family. There are probably

Godparents' Important Role

Just about all Peruvian teens have at least one set of godparents. Parents choose godparents for their children to mark special occasions in their childhood. Usually a person's most important godparents are the ones chosen for his or her baptism. But sets of godparents are also chosen for major events like marriage and a first haircut—an important symbolic ceremony in Peru that usually takes place at about age 1.

Most Peruvian teens have strong relationships with their godparents. Godchildren call their godfather *padrino* and their godmother *madrina*. The children's parents call the godparents *compadre* and *comadre*. If both parents die, the godparents often raise the children.

Parents can choose godparents from inside or outside their families, but they generally choose someone who is well-off. Godparents are not expected to take care of their godchildren financially, but they give gifts at major events like baptisms.

Many poor farm families select a neighboring landowner to be their child's godparents. This forges a lasting bond between the two families despite their different incomes. The connection between godparent and godchild is one of the few links between low-income and wealthier communities.

padrino
pah-DREEN-oh
madrina
mah-DREEN-ah
compadre
cohm-PAH-dray
comadre
cohm-MAH-dray

several reasons for this. In recent decades, there has been a lot of violence related to terrorism in Peru's countryside. The violence has killed many parents and children. There has also been more migration by one parent or the other to a city in search of an escape from poverty. This has increased the number of single-parent families and limited family size.

However, most families in rural areas of Peru remain bound by the need to work hard to feed and shelter themselves. Typically the father is in charge—he even walks ahead of his family on outings to a neighboring village or market—but everybody in the family has a work role. After rural teenagers stop attending school—almost always by age 12 or so—they spend nearly all of their time with their extended family.

A History With Terrorism

Long before terrorism became an everyday concern for many people around the world, Peruvians were dealing with it. Terrorist groups that wanted to take over the government got their start in rural Peru in the 1970s and 1980s. By 1990, they were also active in Peru's cities. A young Peruvian who was 8 years old in 1990 recalls what those years were like:

I remember not having lights because a terrorist group had brought down a power plant. I remember not having water because there were no water-saving plans, no wells that functioned properly. I also recall not having essential items such as milk in the stores. We could only purchase a certain amount of milk per week. Finally, I remember not being allowed out because it was way too dangerous. Nobody could guarantee that a terrorist group wouldn't bomb the movie theater—we weren't even safe at home, for that matter, and school was also canceled a few times. My father had to move out of the country due to violent threats.

47

Looking through garbage to find something that can be sold is common in Peru's shantytowns.

Forming Friendships

The idea of having groups of friends with similar interests is foreign to teens in many parts of rural Peru. Family ties and the hard work needed for daily existence take up all of a teen's time and energy. However, as more teens stay in school longer, they develop friendships with teens from other families. After they leave school, these friendships might fade. But they keep close ties with their extended family.

Teens in urban Peru, however, make and keep friends throughout their lives. Those who grow up in shanty-towns forge close friendships with other teens they meet on the streets or at school. When not busy with family chores, they may spend the day with friends. Without any money to spend, they often make getting money the focus of the day.

A group of teens may search through garbage to find something valuable enough to sell. Uncovering a discarded small appliance or a few cigarettes is considered a big success. The group may spend hours hawking their finds on a street corner. If they are lucky again, and someone pays them a little money for their goods, they can treat themselves to a snack from a street vendor. Yet even though they "earned" the money on their own, many teens would feel an obligation to give it to their families.

Meanwhile, middle- and upper-income teens make friends at school and during after-school activities, such as sports and music lessons. Teens from middle-income families make friends with teens who have similar back-

Teens whose families are not poor can enjoy their free time and luxuries such as digital cameras.

49

grounds. Most have telephones in their homes, and some have cell phones that let them stay in frequent touch with each other. Almost all have televisions and keep up with pop culture around the world. They shop at shopping malls and buy imported clothes, such as T-shirts with logos of their favorite teams or bands. Teen boys have more freedom than girls, who often

Popular Peruvian Names

Girls:	Boys:
Andrea	Alessio
Antonella	Augusto
Chiara	José
Claudia	Lorenzo
Laura	Miguel
Mariella	Rafael
Rocío	Raúl
Romina	Ricardo
Tamaya	Sergio
Wayna	Wayra
Ximena	

Peruvian parents control their daughters more tightly than their sons.

have early curfews and have to tell their parents where they will be.

Teens from wealthy families have lifestyles similar to those of upper-income teens in most of the world. They usually attend exclusive private schools. They often travel to other countries and even go abroad for school. So they are likely to make friends with teens from other countries. They shop at exclusive stores and buy designer clothes from Europe and the United States. But they have one thing in common with all other Peruvian teens: Family comes first.

Feet fly and skirts swirl at the Inti Raymi festival in Cuzco. It draws Peruvians and tourists alike.

4

Many Days & Ways to Celebrate

MUSIC FILLS THE AIR AS MORE THAN A DOZEN traditional and modern bands perform on the streets of Cuzco, the former Inca capital city in the Andes highlands. On one corner, Peruvian folk music rings out as young and old dancers jam the street. The dancers all wear traditional Quechua costumes of white shirts and knitted caps. The women and girls wear colorful, billowing skirts. They all seem to be expert dancers, and to be having fun.

At the other end of the street, a popular local band blasts out a dance hit. Teenagers in their newest jeans and imported fashions show off their dance moves. They are also clearly enjoying themselves. When the band starts another song, new dancers join, and others make their way down another block to hear more music.

It's the biggest day of the year in this city of 400,000 residents. Today, June 24, people from all over Peru and even tourists from other countries have come to Cuzco.

Public Holidays

New Year's Day—January 1
Holy Thursday—Thursday before Easter
Good Friday—Friday before Easter
Easter—March or April
Labor Day—May 1
Day of the Peasant (Inti Raymi and Feast of St. John the Baptist)—June 24
Feast of St. Peter and St. Paul—June 29
Independence Day—July 28
Feast of St. Rose of Lima—August 30
Day of National Dignity—October 8
All Saints' Day—November 1
Immaculate Conception—December 8
Christmas Eve—December 24
Christmas Day—December 25

They are celebrating Inti Raymi, the Inca Festival of the Sun. For nearly 1,000 years, indigenous Peruvians have celebrated this festival as a day to worship the Sun God. According to Inca belief, the sun controls all aspects of plant, animal, and human life.

The festival takes place during the winter solstice, when the sun is farthest from Earth. The traditional festivities included a day of dance, song, and offerings. They were all aimed at persuading the sun to stay longer in the sky, bring a new planting season, and provide more warmth during the winter.

After the Spanish conquered Peru, they tried to eliminate all pagan religions—including Incan beliefs. They wanted to convert all native Peruvians to Catholicism. One method they used was to turn traditional festivals into Catholic religious festivals. Since Inti Raymi happened to fall on the same day of the year as the Feast of St. John

Catholicism

More than eight of 10 Peruvians call themselves Roman Catholic. This religion was brought to Peru by the Spanish, who worked hard to convert as many native Peruvians as they could. Today Catholic Masses are celebrated in the Quechua and Aymará languages to attract indigenous people. But even though so many Peruvians claim to be Catholic, church attendance is low. Only about 15 percent of those who say they are Catholic attend Mass every week.

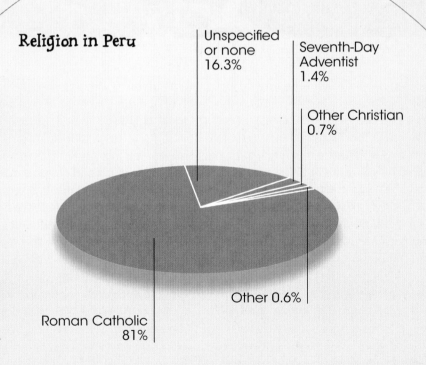

Religion in Peru

Unspecified or none 16.3%

Seventh-Day Adventist 1.4%

Other Christian 0.7%

Other 0.6%

Roman Catholic 81%

Source: United States Central Intelligence Agency. *The World Factbook—Peru.*

Palms are prepared for Palm Sunday, a major Roman Catholic observance.

the Baptist, the conquerors simply combined the two events. They tried to emphasize the Catholic feast day rather than the traditional Inca celebration. Nevertheless, the practice allowed Peruvians to continue following their centuries-old Inti Raymi traditions. Today the festival blends Catholic and Inca traditions. It also mixes modern and ancient styles of music, dance, and celebration.

Before the street music and dancing begins, a group carrying Catholic icons makes its way through the city streets. This is followed by a procession of women who are wearing traditional Inca clothing and bearing

gifts for the Sun God. After this comes the sacrificial "killing" of a llama. The llama isn't really killed, but the ritual imitates the Inca practice of sacrificing a llama on Inti Raymi. This blending of two religions and cultures does not seem odd to Peruvians. It is how they have celebrated ever since the Spanish brought their religion and culture to Peru in the 1500s.

Religious Holidays

Of Peru's 13 public holidays, six are Catholic. All teens—whether they consider themselves religious or not— celebrate on these days. Holy Thursday, Good Friday, and Easter Sunday are all

MANY DAYS & WAYS TO CELEBRATE

part of Semana Santa, or Holy Week. During this week of celebrating the Catholic belief in Jesus Christ's resurrection, festivities take place throughout Peru. Many teens take part in nightly candlelight processions through their town or city. Some festivities include re-enactments of Jesus' crucifixion. The most famous Semana Santa festival is in the town of Ayacucho.

Two other religious holidays are celebrated in Peru's winter months of June, July, and August. The Feast of St. Peter and St. Paul, who were early Christian leaders, takes place on June 29. On August 30, Peruvians celebrate the first person to become a saint in the Americas, St. Rose of Lima. She ran an infirmary at her home for poor children and the elderly.

Local Celebrations

Almost every Peruvian town, city, or village celebrates its own patron saint with a festival that can last up to a week. The patron saints were often chosen by the Spanish conquistadores. They chose saints with birthdays close to the dates of the towns' largest native celebrations. So the indigenous Peruvians continued to celebrate the occasions they were used to celebrating. Today patron saint celebrations often begin with a procession of townspeople carrying a small statue of the patron saint. This is followed by dancing, music, and feasting.

Teens work with their parents and siblings to prepare for these special events. In some villages, the honor—and huge expense—of hosting the celebration is passed from one family to another each year. The hosts plan the events and, with other families, provide the food and drink. In some towns, a church member is elected to plan and raise money for the event. This person is called the majordomo. The majordomo

A figure of St. Peter, the patron saint of fishermen, is escorted in the port of Chorrillos, near Lima, on the feast day of St. Peter and St. Paul.

Traditional clothes are worn in a religious festival in the village of Ollantaytambo.

Summer In January

Peru is below the equator, so the longest days of the year—in the summer, when the weather is warmest—occur in December and January. The shortest days of the year—during Peru's winter—are in June and July: So it's warm during the Christmas and New Year's holidays, but colder during Inti Raymi in June.

plans events such as processions, music, dancing, and fireworks displays. Often there is a *castillo*, which means a fireworks "castle." For a castillo, fireworks are lit from a wooden tower placed in the town square. The resulting displays can be spectacular.

castillo
cah-STEE-yoh

National Holidays

Peruvian teens also get a few nonreligious days off from school—or work—each year. The two most important national holidays are Independence Day on July 28 and the Day of National Dignity, which commemorates a Peruvian naval hero, on October 8.

Independence Day celebrations usually last two days, and teens have no school on July 28 or 29. The date marks the day in 1821 that Peru's Declaration of Independence from Spain was signed by José de San Martín, an Argentine general who fought for and achieved Peru's independence. Some Peruvians fly the national flag outside their homes all of July in celebration of independence. On the eve of Independence Day, people begin celebrating with outdoor music and dancing. On the morning of July 28, cannons fire 21-gun salutes. Later that day, a big military parade is held in downtown Lima and attended by Peru's president. July 29 is often a day of recovery from the previous day's celebrations.

The Day of National Dignity, on October 8, marks a less victorious moment in Peruvian history. On this date in 1879, the Peruvian navy lost the Battle of Angamos to the Chilean navy, and a Peruvian navy commander, Admiral Miguel Grau, was killed.

Quinceañero

Throughout Latin America, a person's 15th birthday calls for a big celebration. In Peru, the celebration is called a quinceañero. (In the rest of Latin America except Puerto Rico, the feminine term quinceañera is used instead.)

From the smallest mountain villages to the elite suburbs of Lima, the quinceañero is a major event in the life of a Peruvian teen. Food, music, and festive dress are always part of the celebration. Wealthy families usually rent a hotel or ballroom, have food catered, and nearly always hire a band. Designer outfits are bought for all family members. A family might even take a daughter to Europe or the United States to find the perfect quinceañero dress. In lower-income families, less money is spent, but the effect is the same: Special clothes, special food and drink, and plenty of music are part of the day.

quinceañero
KEEN-see-ahn-YEH-ro
quinceañera
KEEN-see-ahn-YEH-rah

Many Peruvian teens who have not been able to find work would consider an ice cream vendor lucky to have a job.

5

Working Challenges

PERUVIAN TEENS DO MANY TYPES OF WORK. Sometimes they hold paying jobs, and sometimes they work without pay to produce food for their families. The kind of work they do—like just about everything else in Peru—depends on where they live and their family's social class. In one part of Lima, a well-dressed teenager might spend his after-school hours at his father's workplace, preparing for when he will enter the family business. Just blocks away, another teen may spend her days wheeling an old grocery cart around the city, scouring the streets for

potentially valuable trash. Her family survives by collecting and reselling trash. She cannot take time off to attend school full time in the hope of getting a better job someday.

Peru has an estimated unemployment rate of 7.4 percent. For every 100 people who are able and want to work, about seven cannot find a job. Compared with the jobless rates in most countries, this rate is not high—an unemployment rate of about 4 percent is considered full employment in industrialized countries. If 93 of every 100 Peruvian teenagers could find a good job, the outlook

Three generations of people in a home-based leather workshop in Peru's central highlands

for them would be pretty good. But the United Nations reports that the unemployment rate for Peruvian youths is much higher. In 2001, it was estimated at 13.1 percent. Even this fairly low rate hides the serious unemployment problems faced by teens.

It is hard to measure employment rates in rural Peru. The national unemployment rate reflects only city residents and only people with "documented" jobs—those whose pay is recorded and who pay taxes on their earnings. A huge number of Peruvians work in "informal" employment. In the cities, this means they sell goods on street corners, work in people's homes cleaning or providing other services, or collect garbage on the streets. In the 1990s, more than 90,000 street vendors were selling food in Lima alone, and most of them were mothers or teenagers.

WORKING CHALLENGES

Child labor is a huge problem in these informal jobs. Thousands of young children and teens spend their days performing low-wage, unskilled labor that prevents them from going to school. Peru's government has created several programs aimed at limiting children's working hours and letting them attend school. One law raised the age for entering school from 6 to 9 to accommodate children who could not enter school on time. Another program pays children in Lima up to 320 nuevo soles (U.S. $110) a year to attend school. The money is intended to help families survive without relying on their children.

Another big problem in Peru is underemployment—having a job, but not earning enough to have a decent lifestyle. Such jobs do not take full

Young children are often put to work selling things to help support their families.

63

A 9-year-old girl and her brother, 11, made bricks with the rest of their family. For 1,000 bricks, the family earned about 54 nuevos soles (U.S.$20).

advantage of people's talents and skills. For instance, many recent migrants to cities work as day laborers (workers hired for only a day at a time) at construction sites. They officially have jobs, but they make very little money and perform dangerous and difficult work. It has been estimated that about half of Peruvians are underemployed.

Jobs in Services and Industry

Peru's "official" workers—the number the employment rate is based on—total about 9.4 million. That's only about half of the country's working-age population. Of those workers, nearly three out of four work in service jobs. This includes most office work, as well as tourism, sales, and communications jobs. In recent years, tourism has grown in Peru as travelers from around the world have developed an interest in ecotourism. Such tourists visit natural sites and disturb the environment as little as

Division of Labor in Peru

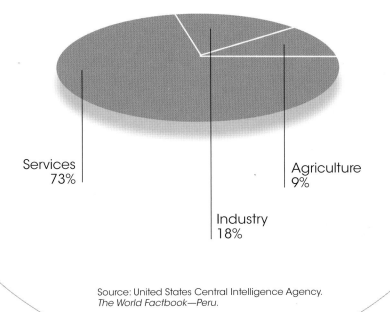

Services
73%

Industry
18%

Agriculture
9%

Source: United States Central Intelligence Agency.
The World Factbook—Peru.

possible. With its
remnants of centuries-
old civilizations and its natural beauty,
Peru is becoming a hot spot for international ecotourists. Many urban teens are
learning to speak English, German, and
French in an effort to gain jobs in the
growing tourist industry.

About one of five
Peruvian workers is employed
in industry. This includes mining,
manufacturing, and construction.
Nearly all construction work is done
in or near Lima and other large cities.
Many teens who have these jobs hope
to find better jobs. Peru's mining

Peruvian farmers have raised smaller numbers of livestock in recent years.

industry is small in terms of jobs but huge in terms of profits. Almost half of the nation's export profits come from mining. In fact, the world's most profitable gold mine, Yanacocha, is in Peru. The country's abundant natural resources also include silver, copper, lead, and zinc. Officially, only about 1 percent of Peruvians work in mining. But since most mining work is not documented—so workers don't pay taxes—it is hard to know how many people work in the mines.

On the Farm

Most rural Peruvian teens have experience with farmwork. Growing crops and tending to livestock are part of everyday life in most areas of the country. Although rural Peru has many independent farmers, fewer than 10 percent of the country's workers hold documented jobs in agriculture. Nearly 80 percent of Peru's agricultural workers either own a small plot of land or farm a communal plot with other community members.

This is the way most teens learn to farm—by working alongside their parents and older relatives on family-owned or community-owned land. But they are not learning modern farming techniques. They are learning to grow crops in much the same way their ancestors did for hundreds of years.

Working in the Mines

Officially, fewer than 1 percent of Peruvian workers have mining jobs. However, most mining work is not regulated or documented. Human-rights groups around the world are concerned that many teens and even young children are performing dangerous and unhealthful jobs in mines. An investigation found that more than 100 children ages 7 to 17 were working in gold mining or processing in southern Peru. Of these children, 76 were boys and 28 were girls. Most worked alongside the rest of their families. They received no pay themselves, but their work contributed to their families' ability to survive. The study found that some teens ages 15 to 17 were living alone and working in gold mining. They were paid very little.

Mining is especially dangerous for children because workers are exposed to large amounts of mercury. This poisonous substance can harm children's developing eyesight, hearing, speech, thinking, and coordination. Peru has laws to limit child labor. And international human-rights workers are trying to end the practice of allowing Peruvian teens and younger children to work in mines.

They use very few machines, and they use animals such as llamas or burros to carry heavy burdens. This limits what they can produce.

Most farm labor is done family by family. A teen works with his immediate family to plant, grow, and harvest crops, as well as to breed livestock such as cattle, llamas, and sheep. Many rural communities rely on a traditional system of shared labor during busy planting and harvest seasons. This work-exchange system is called *minka*. Under minka, extended-family members and neighbors help out on one another's farms when needed.

minka
MEEN-ka

But minka is as much a celebration and a time to socialize with neighbors as it is a working time. The host family provides meals and drinks for all the workers. They are usually prepared by the mother and daughters, while the men and boys work in the fields. Providing food for up to two dozen workers can be a huge task that requires months of preparation. Sometimes the host family even provides musicians to entertain the workers. In the best circumstances, minka workers are able to efficiently complete the work and celebrate with neighbors. Often, though, the celebrating gets in the way of completing the work, so the family needs to hire workers to finish the job.

Top Jobs

Most middle- and upper-income teens begin studying for a career after they graduate from high school. They may go abroad to a university or attend one of the more than 30 colleges and universities in Peru. Engineering, law, and medicine are all considered top-notch careers among Peru's elite. Many teens have known from an early age that they will go into a family business. They can avoid a long job search, because they know they will be hired by someone in the family.

Hiring family members is called nepotism, and it is very common in Peru. It reflects Peruvians' deep connections to their families. It is not considered unfair in Peru to hire only family members. In fact, it is considered unwise to hire anybody outside the family. After all, business owners and managers already know the strengths and weaknesses of their family members. They can place relatives in the jobs they think would be best for them. If they hired an "outsider," they would be taking a gamble that the person would be suitable for the job.

But there are big drawbacks to this family-based hiring system. It is unfair to good workers who do not come from well-connected families. Even if a talented worker gets an entry-level job in a large firm, he or she will probably never be promoted very high. This can prevent new ideas from helping businesses to do well.

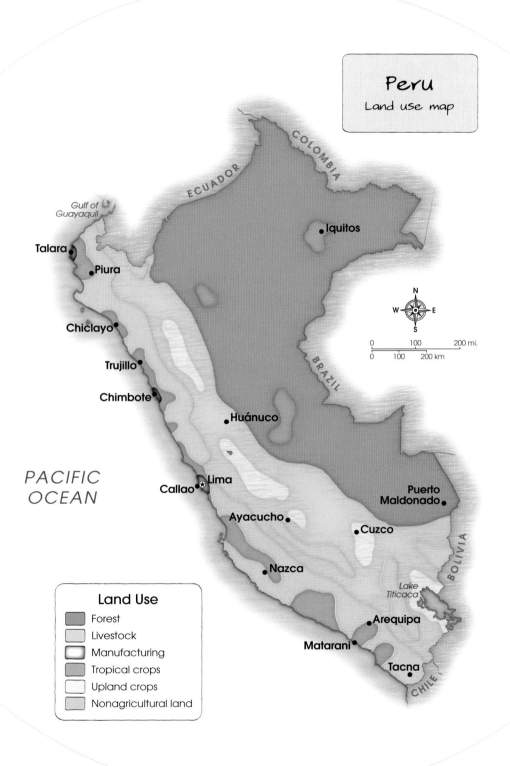

Peru
Land use map

COLOMBIA

ECUADOR

Gulf of
Guayaquil

• Iquitos

Talara •

• Piura

BRAZIL

Chiclayo •

Trujillo •

Chimbote •

• Huánuco

PACIFIC
OCEAN

Callao • ★ • Lima

Puerto
Maldonado •

• Ayacucho

• Cuzco

BOLIVIA

• Nazca

Lake
Titicaca

Land Use

Forest
Livestock
Manufacturing
Tropical crops
Upland crops
Nonagricultural land

• Arequipa

Matarani •

• Tacna

CHILE

N
W   E
S

0   100   200 mi.
0   100   200 km

Soccer has been a popular sport in Peru since at least 1930, when the national team first competed in the FIFA World Cup.

6

Leisure, Often With a Passion

TEENS THROUGHOUT PERU ENJOY a variety of leisure activities. Spectator sports, especially bullfighting and soccer, are huge attractions in both urban and rural Peru. The country's varied geography provides rivers, mountains, and beaches for lots of outdoor recreation as well. And Peruvian teens love nightlife that includes two of their favorite activities—music and socializing.

The sound in the outdoor stadium is deafening. The crowd of 13,000 cheers wildly as a blur of action takes place in the center of the field. Only two national sports, soccer and bullfighting, create this kind of excitement throughout the country. Many Peruvian teens have been to either a bullfight or a soccer game, and almost all can name heroes in both sports.

In Lima, thousands of upper- and middle-income teens attend bullfights with their families each year in the Plaza de Acho. This is the oldest bullfighting stadium in the Americas and the second oldest in the world. Crowds sit in rows of seats circling the vast open-air arena. In rural Peru, bullfights are held in open

Bullfights raise passions at the famous Plaza de Acho stadium in Lima.

fields. Without the steep admission prices charged at arenas, they attract poorer families.

Wherever the event takes place, bullfighting follows a tightly ordered ritual. In the arena, up to three *matadores*, or bullfighters, face six bulls. Each matador has six assistants—two *picadors*, or lancers, mounted on horseback, and three *banderilleros*, or flagmen.

Each matador also has a special assistant to carry his sword. Two others assist the assistants.

The bullfight begins with a parade. Then the picadors enter the ring on horseback and attack

matadores
MAH-tah-doh-res
picadors
PEE-cah-doors
banderilleros
bahn-day-REE-eh-rohs

the bull's shoulders with their lances. Next the banderilleros enter and pierce the bull's neck with long darts. When the bull has been weakened, the matador makes a grand entrance, waving a red cloth on a short stick.

After engaging the bull with the red cloth in a series of dancelike steps, the matador prepares to kill the animal. Most often, he circles the wounded—and angry—bull and stabs between the shoulder blades. In a perfect bullfight, the matador kills the bull instantly. If it takes many stabs to kill the bull, the crowd might jeer and throw things onto the field.

Bullfighting was introduced to Peru by the Spanish, and it quickly grew into a national sport. In recent years, a growing number of teens have openly criticized bullfighting because of its cruelty to the animals. It is not uncommon to see teens holding protest signs outside big matches at Lima's large bullfighting arena. But many Peruvians consider the sport's cultural and traditional aspects more important than concerns about animal abuse.

Another wildly popular sport in Peru also includes animal deaths. Cockfighting, in which two roosters are fitted with sharp spurs on their legs and

Soccer is so popular in Peru that even a team's practice session draws spectators.

Young sandboarders, inspired by snowboarding videos, often try their skills on the very high dunes in Peru's Ica Desert.

encouraged to attack each other until one dies, is extremely popular among poor Peruvians. Cockfights take place nearly every weekend in Lima's Coliseo de Gallos, a cockfighting arena, as well as throughout the countryside.

A less controversial national sport is soccer. Called *fútbol* in Peru, this sport was introduced by British sailors in the 1890s and immediately became popular. Even farmers who work hard 10 hours a day find that playing an evening game of soccer is a good way to unwind. Almost all Peruvian children play soccer, in organized leagues or simply in open fields. As teens, they still

fútbol
FOOHT-bowl

play, but they also follow their favorite professional teams.

The Peruvian national team has qualified for several World Cup games, and it excites crowds throughout the country. In fact, crowds get so excited that violence has erupted at soccer matches. More than 300 spectators were killed in Lima in 1964 when riots broke out after a referee's decision in a match between Argentina and Peru.

Outdoor Enjoyment

With its mix of rivers, sandy coastline, and mountain ranges, Peru provides the perfect setting for many outdoor activities. Fishing is both a sport and a livelihood for many Peruvians, and the Amazon River as well as the Pacific Ocean provide a bounty of all kinds of catches. Yachting is also a favorite sport, and not just among the wealthiest Peruvians. Many families take vacations

One way to enjoy the outdoors is from the seat of a mo-ped.

Many Peruvians enjoy hiking in the country's towering mountains.

by sailing to the Galapagos Islands. The islands, which are volcanic peaks, have many unusual or unique animals and plants. They were visited by the British naturalist Charles Darwin in 1835.

Hiking in the mountains is another favorite family activity. Some families take leisurely weekend trips along paths that wind through the lower Andes Mountains. Others opt for more adventurous mountaineering in high-altitude areas. The Andes have more than 30 peaks above 20,000 feet (6,096 meters) and provide spectacular views. Groups

Peru
Topographical
map

COLOMBIA

Putumayo River

Napo River

Tigre River

Pastaza River

Gulf of
Guayaquil

ECUADOR

Iquitos

Amazon River

Amazon River Valley

Piura

A
N
D
E
S

Marañón River

Ucayali River

La Selva (Jungle)

BRAZIL

N
W   E
S

0   100   200 mi.
0   100   200 km

Trujillo

Nevado Huascarán

Cordillera Oriental

Nevado Yerupaja

M
O
U
N
T
A
I
N
S

Madre de Dios River

Lima

Cordillera Occidental

Machu Picchu

Cuzco

BOLIVIA

PACIFIC
OCEAN

Nazca

La Costa (Desert)

Lake Titicaca

El Misti

Arequipa

CHILE

⸺ Pan-American Highway

of teens often get together informally or through hiking clubs to take advantage of the country's mountain paths.

Peru's sandy beaches are favorite teen hangouts. The best are south of Lima and are frequented by middle- and upper-income teens from the city. On most weekend days, several beach volleyball games are going on at the same time. During the day, groups of teens swim, sunbathe, and hang out together along the sandy stretches. In the evening, discos and clubs along the shore come alive.

Nightlife

Hitting the discos is popular among wealthy teens. Dance clubs can be found in the cities and beach areas along Peru's coast. Inside, the scene is similar to that of clubs around the world: throbbing pop music, crowds of teens and young adults, and a lot of energy. Teens usually come to clubs in groups of girls and boys. Even if a couple is on a date at night, they usually go out with other friends.

Middle-income teens may also hit the clubs, but usually for special occasions. The cost of admission and drinks is too high for them to go every night. In Lima and other cities, they gather at coffeehouses and movie theaters on weekend evenings.

A special kind of music, *chicha* music, was born in the shantytowns of Lima in the 1960s, and it flourished. Today it is popular among low-income teens. The music is named for the corn beer that is drunk by many poor Peruvians. The style blends rock music with traditional music from the highlands, where many shantytown residents originally came from. Chicha bands almost always include electric guitars and synthesizers, as well as traditional instruments like conga drums. Teens in particular can relate to chicha lyrics. They usually describe love and relationships or touch on the political aspects of being poor and displaced.

Local Lingo

Peruvian teenagers often exclaim "*En buena onda!*" when they see something they like. The phrase literally means "Good wave!" but teenagers use it for "Cool!"

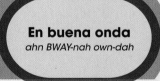

En buena onda
ahn BWAY-nah own-dah

chicha
CHEE-cha

Hanging Out

An upper-income teen from Lima described to a U.S. interviewer how he spends time with his friends on weekends:

During summer we go to beaches an hour south of Lima, and party at the discos there. I also windsurf so I might go to the Bay of Paracas, three hours south of Lima, as well. During winter, we pretty much stay in Lima. There are good nightclubs. During school times, I enjoy going to the movies and hanging out with friends, going out for ice cream, etc. Pretty much throughout the year, I'll go on hiking or photographing trips, as these are two of my hobbies.

Peruvian singer Susana Baca is a performer in the Afro-Peruvian style.

In smaller towns and in Cuzco, the capital city of the highlands area, teens usually go to more traditional events with their families. Every evening event is bound to include music, whether it's Top 40 songs or folk music. Most small villages have a gathering spot where musicians show up nightly and perform for crowds.

Cuzco is dotted with nightclubs. Bands often make the rounds of these clubs, playing a set (a group of songs) in one club and then moving on to the next. Teens and their families might visit a club on a Saturday night and stay to hear four or five bands. If someone has a favorite band, the group might follow the band from club to club, catching a

set at each stop. Sometimes the bands are informal groups of friends, who just enjoy playing together. Usually they are self-taught and are not paid. Some clubs ban roaming bands. Instead they hire a club band for the evening. These bands are usually professional musicians who often write their own music and perform traditional Andean music.

Another popular musical style in Peru is called Afro-Peruvian. It reflects the experiences of African slaves who were brought to Peru in the 1500s, and it has become a source of national pride. Performers such as Perú Negro, Eva Ayllón, and Susana Baca are helping the lively style gain international recognition and popularity.

"El Ambulante" [The Street Seller]

The lyrics to this popular chicha song describe the alienation felt by Lima's poorest residents, who often sell small items on the streets:

Ay, ay, ay, how sad it is to live
How sad it is to dream
I'm a street seller, I'm a proletarian
Selling shoes, selling food, selling jackets
I support my home

Looking Ahead

TEENS IN PERU LIVE IN A RAPIDLY CHANGING WORLD. In some ways, their lives are still defined by the income, class, and racial divisions that are so ingrained in Peruvian culture. Low-income teens continue to struggle to find time to work and attend school. Middle- and upper-income teens continue to live in a relatively isolated world with access to brand-name consumer items and private schools, and with good career prospects.

But these differences are beginning to fade. The government's commitment to education is opening schools to more young Peruvians. Attempts are under way to reduce urban overcrowding and limit child labor. More jobs are being created outside the mining and farming industries. Perhaps today's low-income teens will have more opportunities for a better life than their parents had.

All of Peru's teens—no matter what their background—share a love and respect of family and an appreciation for the chance to celebrate with friends and music. In the future, they will need to work together to improve their country's economy while preserving their sense of family and their rich traditions.

83

Official name: Republic of Peru

Capital: Lima

People

Population: 28,674,757

Population by age group:
0–14 years: 30.3%
15–64 years: 64.2%
65 years and over: 5.4%

Life expectancy at birth: 70 years

Official language: Spanish and Quechua

Other common languages: Aymará and minor Amazonian languages

Religion:
Roman Catholic: 81%
Unspecified or none: 16.3%
Seventh-Day Adventist: 1.4%
Other Christian: 0.7%
Other: 0.6%

Legal ages:
Alcohol consumption: 18
Driver's license: 18
Employment: 14
Leave school: 12
Marriage: 16
Military service: 18
Voting: 18

Government

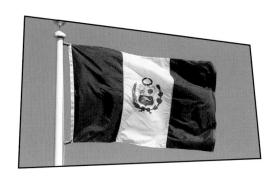

Type of government: Constitutional republic

Chief of state: President, elected by popular vote for five-year term

Head of government: President

Lawmaking body: Unicameral Congress of the Republic of Peru, elected by popular vote

Administrative divisions: 25 regions and one province

Independence: July 28, 1821 (from Spain)

National flag: Three equal vertical bands of red, white, and red; a coat of arms in the center, under a green wreath and flanked by another wreath, features a shield bearing a vicuña, a cinchona tree, and a yellow cornucopia spilling out gold and silver coins

Geography

Total Area: 514,088 square miles (1,285,220 square kilometers)

Climate: Varies from tropical in the east to desert in the west; temperate to frigid in the Andes Mountains

Highest point: Nevado Huascaran, 22,334 feet (6,768 meters)

Lowest point: Pacific Ocean, sea level

Major rivers and lakes: Amazon, Napo, Tigre, and Pastaza rivers; Lake Titicaca

Major landforms: Andes Mountains, Pacific Ocean coast, jungle

Economy

Currency: Nuevo sol

Population below poverty line: 53%

Major natural resources: Copper, silver, gold, lead, zinc, petroleum, timber, fish, iron ore, coal, phosphate, potash, hydropower, natural gas

Major agricultural products: Asparagus, coffee, cotton, sugarcane, rice, potatoes, corn, plantains, grapes, oranges, coca, poultry, beef, dairy products, fish, guinea pigs

Major exports: Copper, gold, zinc, crude petroleum and petroleum products, coffee, potatoes, asparagus, textiles, guinea pigs

Major imports: Petroleum and petroleum products, plastics, machinery, vehicles, iron and steel, wheat, paper

Historical Timeline

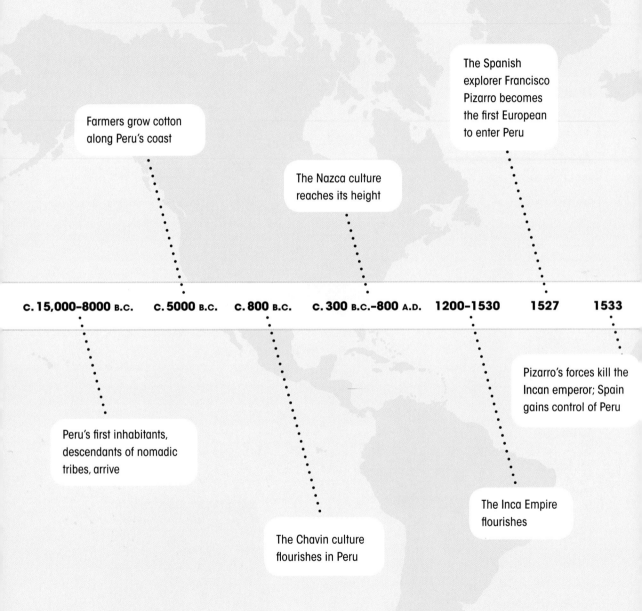

Farmers grow cotton along Peru's coast

The Nazca culture reaches its height

The Spanish explorer Francisco Pizarro becomes the first European to enter Peru

c. 15,000–8000 B.C.   **c. 5000 B.C.**   **c. 800 B.C.**   **c. 300 B.C.–800 A.D.**   **1200–1530**   **1527**   **1533**

Peru's first inhabitants, descendants of nomadic tribes, arrive

The Chavin culture flourishes in Peru

The Inca Empire flourishes

Pizarro's forces kill the Incan emperor; Spain gains control of Peru

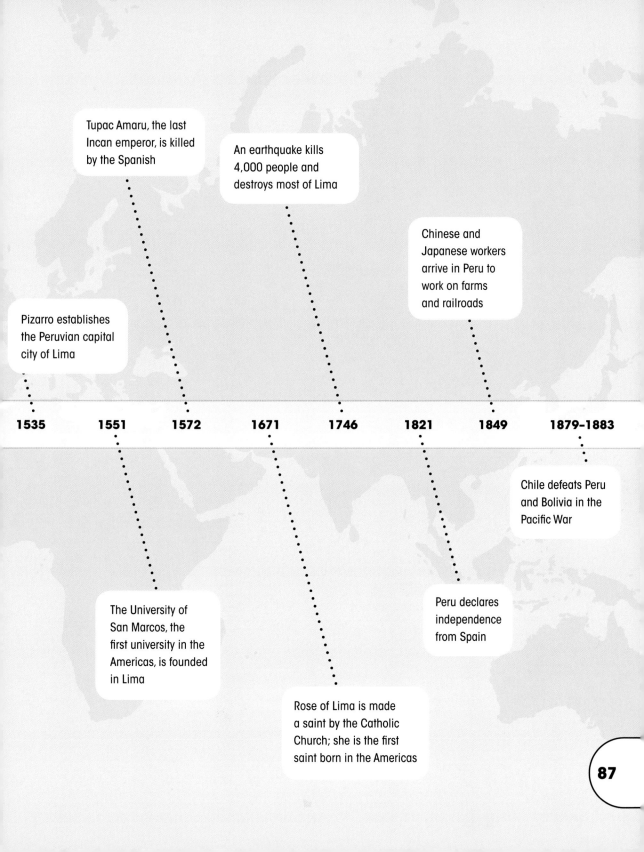

Tupac Amaru, the last Incan emperor, is killed by the Spanish

An earthquake kills 4,000 people and destroys most of Lima

Chinese and Japanese workers arrive in Peru to work on farms and railroads

Pizarro establishes the Peruvian capital city of Lima

1535 **1551** **1572** **1671** **1746** **1821** **1849** **1879–1883**

Chile defeats Peru and Bolivia in the Pacific War

The University of San Marcos, the first university in the Americas, is founded in Lima

Peru declares independence from Spain

Rose of Lima is made a saint by the Catholic Church; she is the first saint born in the Americas

Historical Timeline

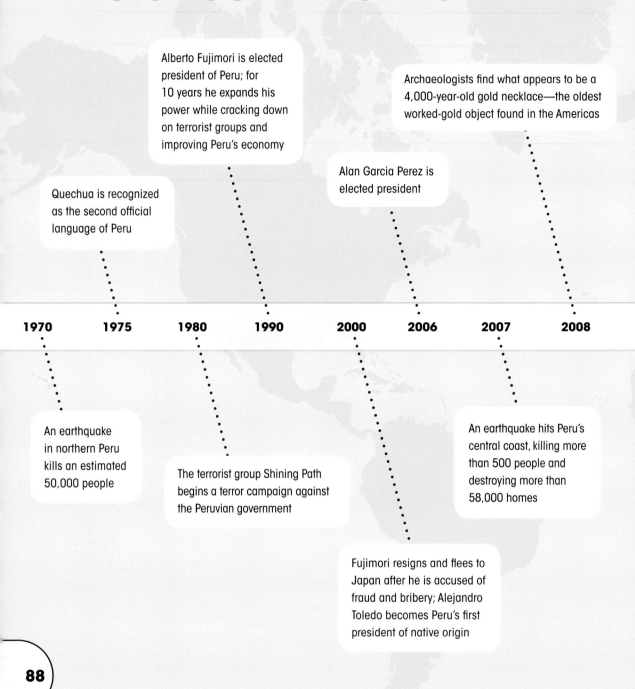

Alberto Fujimori is elected president of Peru; for 10 years he expands his power while cracking down on terrorist groups and improving Peru's economy

Archaeologists find what appears to be a 4,000-year-old gold necklace—the oldest worked-gold object found in the Americas

Alan Garcia Perez is elected president

Quechua is recognized as the second official language of Peru

1970   1975   1980   1990   2000   2006   2007   2008

An earthquake in northern Peru kills an estimated 50,000 people

The terrorist group Shining Path begins a terror campaign against the Peruvian government

An earthquake hits Peru's central coast, killing more than 500 people and destroying more than 58,000 homes

Fujimori resigns and flees to Japan after he is accused of fraud and bribery; Alejandro Toledo becomes Peru's first president of native origin

Glossary

conquistadores | Spanish explorers and soldiers who conquered the Americas

controversial | something about which people disagree

documented | recorded, often by the government

elite | people who have special advantages and privileges

Hispanic | coming from, or related to, countries where Spanish is spoken

icons | images or statues of holy figures

Incas | native people who built a very large South American empire with a capital in Peru

indigenous | related to people who have lived in an area from the earliest times

Latin America | all of the countries south of the United States whose languages are based on Latin, especially Spanish and Portuguese

mercury | poisonous, silvery liquid metal

migration | movement from one region to another

procession | group of people moving along a route as part of an event

proletarian | member of the laboring class

provincial | related to a province, a section of a country

vicuña | animal related to the llama

Additional Resources

IN THE LIBRARY
Fiction and nonfiction titles to further
enhance your introduction to teens in Peru,
past and present.

Abelove, Joan. *Go and Come Back*.
New York: Puffin Books, 2000.

Clark, Ann Nolan. *Secret of the Andes*.
New York: Puffin Books, 1976.

Kravetz, Nathan. *The Way of the
Condor*. Lincoln, Neb.: iUniverse
Inc., 2000.

Eagen, James. *The Aymara of South
America*. Minneapolis: Lerner
Publications, 2002.

Heisey, Janet. *Peru*. Milwaukee:
Gareth Stevens Pub., 2001.

Katz, Samuel M. *Raging Within:
Ideological Terrorism*. Minneapolis:
Lerner Publications, 2004.

Somervill, Barbara A. *Francisco
Pizarro: Conqueror of the Incas*.
Minneapolis: Compass Point
Books, 2005.

ON THE WEB
For more information on this topic,
use FactHound.
1. Go to www.facthound.com
2. Type in this book ID: 0756538521
3. Click on the Fetch It button.

Look for more Global Connections books.

Teens in Australia	*Teens in France*	*Teens in Morocco*	*Teens in Spain*
Teens in Brazil	*Teens in Ghana*	*Teens in Nepal*	*Teens in Turkey*
Teens in Canada	*Teens in India*	*Teens in Nigeria*	*Teens in the U.S.A.*
Teens in China	*Teens in Iran*	*Teens in the Philippines*	*Teens in Venezuela*
Teens in Cuba	*Teens in Israel*	*Teens in Russia*	*Teens in Vietnam*
Teens in Egypt	*Teens in Japan*	*Teens in Saudi Arabia*	
Teens in England	*Teens in Kenya*	*Teens in South Africa*	
Teens in Finland	*Teens in Mexico*	*Teens in South Korea*	

Source Notes

Page 36, column 1, line 7: "The Buzz: Peru Elections." *The NewsHour With Jim Lehrer.* 10 March 2008. www.pbs.org/newshour/extra/editorials/jan-june00/peru_4-11.html

Page 47, sidebar, column 1, line 11: Ibid.

Page 79, column 1, line 5: Ibid.

Pages 84–85, At a Glance: United States. Central Intelligence Agency. *The World Factbook—Peru.* 28 April 2008. https://www.cia.gov/library/publications/the-world-factbook/geos/pe.html

Select Bibliography

"2 Million in Child Labor in Peru." *The Lima Bean*. 13 March 2007. 28 April 2008. http://perunews.wordpress.com/2007/03/13/child-labor-and-education/

Bolin, Inge. *Growing Up in a Culture of Respect: Child Rearing in Highland Peru*. Austin: University of Texas Press, 2006.

Feldman, Heidi. *Black Rhythms of Peru: Reviving African Musical Heritage in the Black Pacific*. Middletown, Conn.: Wesleyan University Press, 2006.

Higgins, James. *Lima: A Cultural History*. New York: Oxford University Press, 2005.

Holligan de Diaz-Limaco, Jane. *Peru: A Guide to the People, Politics and Culture*. New York: Interlink Books, 1998.

Hudson, Rex A., ed. *Peru: A Country Study*. Washington, D.C.: U.S. Government Printing Office, 1992.

International Labour Organization. *Child Labour in Small-Scale Mining: Examples from Niger, Peru & Philippines*. 10 March 2008. 28 April 2007. www.ilo.ch/public/english/dialogue/sector/papers/childmin/137e2.htm#2

Kirk, Robin. *The Monkey's Paw: New Chronicles from Peru*. Amherst: University of Massachusetts Press, 1997.

Norwegian U.N. Association, UNEP/GRID-Arendal, UNU/Global Virtual University, the University College of Hedmark, and INTIS schools. *Globalis—Peru*. http://globalis.gvu.unu.edu/country.cfm?country=PE

"Peru Elections: A Peruvian Teen Is Interviewed by an American High School Newspaper Team." *The NewsHour With Jim Lehrer*. 10 March 2008. www.pbs.org/newshour/extra/editorials/jan-june00/peru_4-11.html

Peterson, Anna, Manuel Vasquez, and Philip Williams, eds. *Christianity, Social Change, and Globalization in the Americas.* New Brunswick, N.J.: Rutgers University Press, 2001.

Skidmore, Thomas E., and Peter H. Smith. *Modern Latin America.* New York: Oxford University Press, 2005.

Starn, Orin., et. al., eds. *The Peru Reader: History, Culture, Politics.* Durham, N.C.: Duke University Press, 2005.

United States Central Intelligence Agency. *The World Factbook—Peru.* 10 March 2008. https://www.cia.gov/library/publications/the-world-factbook/geos/pe.html

United States Department of State. *Background Note: Peru.* 14 May 2008. www.state.gov/r/pa/ei/bgn/35762.htm#travel

Index

About the Author
Sandy Donovan

Sandy Donovan has written many books for young readers. She has also worked as a newspaper reporter, magazine editor, and Web site developer. She has an undergraduate degree in journalism and political science, and a master's degree in labor policy. She lives in Minneapolis, Minnesota, with her family: Fergus, Henry, and Eric.

About the Content Adviser
Jose Javier Lopez, Ph.D.

Our content adviser for *Teens in Peru*, Jose Javier Lopez, is a professor in the Department of Geography at Minnesota State University, Mankato. He is an experienced middle school, high school, and college-level book reviewer, and his research interests include social and economic geography and Latin America. He has a doctorate in geography from Indiana State University.